VISION DISTURBANCE

Christina Masciotti

BROADWAY PLAY PUBLISHING INC
224 E 62nd St, NY, NY 10065
www.broadwayplaypub.com
info@broadwayplaypub.com

First printing: March 2015
I S B N: 978-0-88145-630-1

Book design: Marie Donovan
Page make-up: Adobe Indesign
Typeface: Palatino
Printed and bound in the U S A

VISION DISTURBANCE premiered at Abrons Arts Center on 1 September 2010, presented by New York City Players. The cast and creative contributors were as follows:

MONDO..Linda Mancini
DR HULL...Jay Smith

Director.. Richard Maxwell
Set & lights ....Adrian W Jones
Costumes.. Victoria Vazquez
Sound .... Ben Williams

CHARACTERS

MONDO, *a spirited Greek woman in her early fifties, adrift in Reading, PA; an appreciator of fine tailoring on a modest budget.*

DR HULL, *the town eccentric, in his forties, glumly carrying on his father's practice. He wears long-faded colors, and a Blackberry clipped to his belt.*

(Enveloped by darkness, MONDO *sits in an examination chair.* DR HULL *hovers just in front of her.)*

DR HULL: Watch my light. Follow it as much as you can.

(Near MONDO's *left eye, a handheld pinpoint of light moves around in a circle, casting a haunting, ten foot shadow of her tightly-bunned head. The light clicks off. Full lights come on illuminating a plywood floor with monotonous waves of grain variations and dark knots peering out. A few feet back from the slightly raised edge of the plywood floor is a rigidly upright wall, also plywood, with the same patterns and discolorations; in fact, it almost appears to be an extension of floor, folded up into a confining, plywood box. She is seated in a black chair at the center, suddenly exposed as if pinned down on a dissecting tray.* DR HULL *stands near an identical chair. Stage left, just off the edge of the floor, a cymbal gleams on the otherwise bare stage with a makeshift drumstick, a chair leg, at its base. A decrepit piano, with a small box on the closed keyguard, abuts the stage right edge of the floor.)*

DR HULL: How'd you find me?

MONDO: The Reading Hospital. *(Pause)* I don't remember what's his name is. Doctor Gor—. Let me think. Doctor Argourilis. The Greeks recommended him. You know him? *(Pause)* Must be new. Was very nervous. Was shaking when he was touching me. He said that you were suh-specialist.

DR HULL: Did you say suspicious?

MONDO: Specialist.

DR HULL: Looks like you have a lot going on here, Ms Dimitriades.

MONDO: Mondo. *(Pause)* Mondo, people call me.

DR HULL: Mondo. That short for something?

MONDO: Diamondo.

DR HULL: Like diamond?

MONDO: The girl's best friend, yes.

DR HULL: How long has your eye been bothering you?

MONDO: Two weeks about.

DR HULL: How did it start?

MONDO: Well. Two weeks ago, I woke up and my husband wasn't there. It was very early so I wondered where was he. I was just lying down, staring at a corner of the sheet. It has a pattern of antique roses on it. And out of nowhere, I felt like something was wrong. I didn't know what that was all about, but right away I realized parts of the roses were missing. I mean, there was part of a rose, then a gray thing, then the other part of the rose. Then I looked up, and the chest of drawers was the same, like someone took a hammer—

DR HULL: I got it. Dream-like distortions.

MONDO: Dreeam? Was nightmare. The whole room, everything was pieces. I didn't know what was happening. I didn't think it was my eyes. I thought the house was falling apart, and it scared the hell out of me. The floor was not level, I had to balance myself. I was ready to die. Ready to jump. I went to the emergency to see if my brain took off. Oh gosh.

DR HULL: I'm going to take a look at the back of your eye. Look over my shoulder. *(Pulling his chair closer to hers)* Sit front. Up a little. Rest your chin. *(Beginning the exam)* I never heard the name Diamondo before.

MONDO: Well, there are better stones to be named after. The ruby, the jade, the colors. Diamonds are overexposed. Bad stories behind them. The way they came from other countries. Did you see that movie?

DR HULL: *(No idea what she's talking about)* Right.

MONDO: That's a sad story.

DR HULL: Have you experienced any pain with this?

MONDO: Yes, it hit me like a brick on the head, the pain.

DR HULL: You get migraines?

MONDO: Many times. *(Pause)* I never had a migraine like this before.

(DR HULL *switches to* MONDO's *left eye.)*

DR HULL: I'd like to run an angiogram.

MONDO: A what?

DR HULL: Angiogram.

MONDO: They did that already.

DR HULL: Who?

MONDO: At the hospital. The K G B.

DR HULL: The K G B.

MONDO: Yes, they put me on a table, put jelly, add wires, watch the computer, white lines, green lines. I thought I need a triple quantiple bypass, but they told me, I'm fine.

DR HULL: No. This is different. This is a diagnostic fluorescein angiogram. I'm going to inject a dye to track the blood flow. It'll show me how your heart's working in conjunction with your eyes. Tilt your head back.

(DR HULL *tilts* MONDO's *chair back to a reclined position.*
Blackout. His pen-light comes on. Only her face is visible
under the light.)

DR HULL: Can you see the light?

MONDO: I can't. I can't see!

DR HULL: Give it a chance to wear off.

MONDO: Maybe nuts bother me. Red sauce. Some
allergy. I have some teethache, but I'm not going to
the dentist. That's stress, all the stress went there, too.
My body is tied in nuts and bolts. How would you
feel, you find out your husband, your thirteen years
husband—

DR HULL: Can you see the light?

MONDO: I see. I see now, yes. I had the feeling, but
I didn't wanna believe. He would disappear, phone
turned off. Goes to her house. Comes back, sleeps on
the couch. I know this is a wrong flag, but I was not a
hundred percent. Sometimes if you have needs you do
some wishful thinking. I thought he was the other half
of the orange.

DR HULL: Just keep focusing on that light.

MONDO: He is a contractor, you know, contracts, he
was always working. He started a job at the house of
a lady from the Dominican Republic or Puerto Rican
Colombia, some kind of Colombia. She wears sneakers
with a Puerto Rico thing on the back. All I know is she
doesn't wear shoes. She wears sneakers and on the
back is a Puerto Rico flag.

DR HULL: Don't blink.

MONDO: I would say, "Why are you coming home so
late?" And he would start saying stupid things: he
doesn't have curfew, he's a grown man.

DR HULL: Open your eye.

MONDO: I graduated from community school, he didn't come, he came after, he said, listen now, lies: he was sick all day, he couldn't come. He brought me balloons, and big box with five pastries that they move back and forth and ups and downs. Very stingy guy. Doesn't spend. And he put the shades down right away so I couldn't see he came with her car. So I told him, I want you to stop seeing this person. He said, "That's not easy, I have my expensive tools there." He has his tools there, all this stupid stuff he says. I told him stop working there, take your tools! He says, "How can I do this? I promised to be there for her to support her kids." That's what he tells me.

(The pen-light clicks off. Blackout.)

MONDO: He tells me how bad a wife I am. I don't know how to treat a man. I didn't love him because I didn't iron his underwear. That was tough, folks. I was in this situation, I spent all these years. Now he says all these stupid things.

(Full lights come on. MONDO's chair has been restored to an upright position. DR HULL stands near her.)

DR HULL: You just noticed this two weeks ago?

MONDO: Yes.

DR HULL: See these two spots?

MONDO: Yes.

DR HULL: They're on your retina. The small one's probably been there a few months. And the big one, even longer. That's a cause for concern because it's encroaching on the optic nerve.

MONDO: Oh.

DR HULL: Idiopathic Central Serous Chorioretinopathy.

MONDO: That's the name?

DR HULL: What you have basically is a leak. These spots are two sacks where internal fluid is collecting. There's a leaking of pigment on your retina.

MONDO: Is it genetic or something?

DR HULL: Hard to say. Studies suggest stress is the trigger.

MONDO: Stress?

DR HULL: Those ruthless, obsessive, Type A personalities. That's where you see this. Investment bankers. Usually men. It's a preservative reflex. Forces you to rest.

MONDO: So, I'm too triple A personality?

DR HULL: What?

MONDO: Is stress?

DR HULL: Stress. That's right. Have you been under a lot of stress lately?

MONDO: No.

DR HULL: Can you describe your lifestyle?

MONDO: Whatever it is, I love it.

DR HULL: What do you do for a living?

MONDO: Work at the community college.

DR HULL: Doing what?

MONDO: Institutional Affairs. Give the forms for I Ds and enter on the computer. Everybody has something to say. Keeps sending me emails. I have lotsa stuff to do, tons, tons, tons. Zillion billion stuff. And my supervisor doesn't want to work, she wants to eat potato chips. She's gonna eat three thirds of that bag while she looks for me to do her things. I think she tries to get rid of me. She doesn't say to my face. Behind me. I feel like she scapegoats me. *(Pause)* Could it happen to my other eye?

DR HULL: Unlikely. I mean anything could happen, but your right eye's not showing any signs of a problem. That's actually what's causing your headaches. Each of your eyes is sending a different image to your brain. One is crystal clear, the other's warped.

MONDO: How do you treat it?

DR HULL: There is no treatment.

MONDO: Nothing?

DR HULL: You'll need to be monitored every few weeks to make sure the sacks are getting smaller.

MONDO: You can't cure it?

DR HULL: There is no cure, but it is curable.

MONDO: I asked you a basic questions and I got a trick answer.

DR HULL: Hah! *(His mild exclamation sends a jolt through his back)* There are more than five hundred ways this could go. There's a sixty percent chance you'll regain twenty/twenty acuity. We just have to wait it out. *(Pause)* There is also the option of surgery. It's called focal laser photo-coagulation. It repairs the R P E at the site of the leakage. However, I'd only consider it if this doesn't resolve itself in a reasonable period of time.

MONDO: How long's that gonna take?

DR HULL: Usually, it clears itself up over a period of months.

MONDO: Months! It's gonna take all that much time?

DR HULL: Could only be weeks. There's no real timetable.

MONDO: In other words you don't have idea.

DR HULL: Every human being is different.

MONDO: Oh gosh.

DR HULL: There are steps you can take to speed healing.

MONDO: Like if I stop drinking? Or have the fat cheese free instead? I made a New Year's Eve resolution to start with the pink sugar. And avoid bread. I usually remove the flesh, and I eat the crust. Will that help?

DR HULL: Have a drink if it relaxes you.

MONDO: Even Frangelica?

DR HULL: Whatever you want.

MONDO: I know red wine makes the blood smooth, but Frangelica wakes up all your taste buds.

DR HULL: The most important thing you can do is relax.

MONDO: That's it? There's nothing else I can do?

DR HULL: Is there anything you like to do? Anything fun, anywhere you like to go?

(Pause)

MONDO: I like to go to the symphony. This is one of my favorite things. I love this classic music.

DR HULL: Season tickets?

MONDO: Pardon?

(DR HULL takes a prescription pad out of his back pocket.)

DR HULL: I have partial season tickets. *(Writing)* They have a great Tchaikovsky series coming up. You should go.

(He rips off her prescription and gives it to her.)

MONDO: *(Reading)* Magnificat? *(Pause)* I don't pay for names. The generic of this is fine for me.

DR HULL: It's not a pill. It's a cantata. Bach.

MONDO: Pardon?

DR HULL: I prefer the *Mass in B Minor*.

MONDO: That's my prescription? Music?

DR HULL: For a hysterical reaction, absolutely.

MONDO: This piece of paper is giving me a hysterical reaction. I'm ready to scream—

DR HULL: No, no. Have you ever heard about hysterical reactions?

MONDO: Who?

DR HULL: You're seizing up over tension. Music can help you release that tension. Especially, classical music because of the rhythms. It goes up, comes down, races, stops dead. That's all in your body, too, all the same rhythms, that's why your body responds—

MONDO: I'm not coming to you for lessons of music, you know this?

DR HULL: Ms Dimitriades, you have to listen to me.

MONDO: Loud and clear, but I have a feeling you do not listen to me. I have a serious problem here, it cannot be going on for months, it's a jumpy situation.

DR HULL: I know.

MONDO: So I should listen to Prince? I have *Chocolate Rain*, how many times I need to play that?

DR HULL: I'm trying to help you.

MONDO: I'm sorry, but I don't believe in fantasytale stories. I am reality period. Reality. Sometimes you have to be real with people, you have to just hit them over the head.

DR HULL: All right. You heard what I think. If you're not interested, I can refer you to another specialist who takes your insurance.

MONDO: You're the only one in Berks. Others are in Baltimore, others are New Jersey. How I'm gonna get there? I cannot drive with my eye.

DR HULL: I would start by walking to the symphony this Thursday.

(Classical music starts to play. MONDO stands.)

MONDO: Time to relax, folks. *(Sarcastic)* According to my doctor, I cannot let go another day without music. *(She picks up her chair and places it on the forward edge of the plywood floor.)* First of all, I don't like American music. It doesn't deal with the whole gamoot of emotions. Greece, music carries history of country, dictatorship, history of individuals, songs who are very, who satirize politics, have some myths. Here, I don't think there's a song about Washington or Roosevelt. *(Sitting)* There are some rituals I miss. Go to all the concerts, have all these great musicians, songs and lyrics. This music, about life. Pain, leaving family, labor, how hard their lives. People you love. How you earn your bread. How you need to find for your love. All these traditions, gypsy music, North Africa, Balkan peninsula mixed together. All this gamoot of emotions. The lyrics were complicated at least. People connected all together. We sing. We become a whole thing there. Greeks have spirit, wit, they're very sarcastic. They have this self-sarcasm. Sarcasm means some depth.

(The music seems to burst apart, becoming a chaos of different instruments and ultimately a kind of deafening buzz.)

MONDO: Bad idea, folks. *(She gets up and carries her chair back to DR HULL.)*

(March)

(DR HULL is seated near MONDO.)

MONDO: Are the spots getting smaller?

DR HULL: *(Rubbing his eyes)* They're not getting bigger.

MONDO: What's wrong?

DR HULL: Sorry. My cat had kittens last night. Long night.

MONDO: I want to have the laser. *(Pause)* There is a laser surgery, you told me. *(Pause)* I want to have it. I don't wanna wait for this to go away, it's not going. I feel shaky all the time. I never know what's on this side, I have to turn my head constantly.

DR HULL: It's only been a few weeks.

MONDO: I know you said my condition will probably cure by itself, but I cannot live like this. I have to appear in court, I cannot appear like this. My husband is fighting me.

DR HULL: Are you in the process of a divorce?

MONDO: Yes.

DR HULL: Was that a sudden decision?

MONDO: It was my decision.

DR HULL: That would explain the stress.

MONDO: If you think that's the solution and that's the problem, think again.

DR HULL: You don't think your divorce had something to do with it?

MONDO: The marriage was more nervewrecking than the divorce.

DR HULL: Divorce puts a huge strain on a person. Getting over it, finding a sense of closure—

MONDO: I don't need the closure. If someone walks out on you, that's the closure. What about the surgery?

DR HULL: Chorioretinopathy is a psycho-physiological event. It runs a parallel course with your feelings.

Laser treatment is not indicated. The risks outweigh
the benefits at your age.

MONDO: I'm too old?

DR HULL: Too young!

MONDO: I'm fifty-one.

DR HULL: I know. That's young. The median age for
focal laser coagulation is seventy-five. Sixty five's the
lowest end of the spectrum.

MONDO: Why?

DR HULL: The surgery can hold up for twenty years.
Beyond that is speculation. I'm not willing to risk
serious complications, especially when this will
typically heal itself.

MONDO: But I'm not in a shape where I can present
myself. I can lose my house. How I'm gonna go to the
trial like this?

DR HULL: I recommend Beethoven's *Egmont Overture.*

(*Classical music starts to play.* MONDO *stands up, and
starts taking uncertain steps toward the back wall.*)

MONDO: When you deal with the legal system it's
scary, folks. Because you realize there is no justice
there. You're right, but you cannot prove anything.
We agreed before the court that I would keep the
house. I offered to pay him six thousand dollars, he
says it's worth more money, it's close to a historical
district. Vinyl siding. You can hear it flapping. It's like
living in a tree. They're not gonna put it in the historic
book, our house. He wants eight thousand. Oh gosh.
So I wrote him a check, eight thousand dollars, so
it's out of my way. Then he says in court, listen now,
he's with someone else, he says he has the kind of
wife who doesn't support him. Judge told me to say
something, I told the Judge, horrible macho judge,

Wilbur Smith. I told him, I don't confess to know
the law, but I couldn't afford to have a lawyer, that's
why I was myself. *(She has arrived at the upstage right
corner, near the piano. She picks up the small box from the
piano, opens it, takes out a black eye patch, and puts it on
as she speaks.)* My husband's lawyer, said my husband
was victim. I start to talk, Judge made faces. With me
he made face, he didn't listen. But he listened to my
husband. If I argued the way he did, I'd be in prison.
My husband said he asked for his wife to help him and
I didn't. I said, yes I did, I gave a check for the house.
He looked at me in the eyes and said he never saw the
check. That dropped the cake. The Judge was about
to call someone to find out if he ever got the check,
and my husband says, "I think I remember I received
something." He lied! In court! Because he lied, I kept
my house, folks.

*(The music begins to disintegrate into an arbitrary
succession of irritating sounds.)*

MONDO: But he had another house, besides the one we
lived. On the top of everything, he's a junk collector.
He was possessed of the junk collecting. He had fines
from the other house from codes. The house is like a
garage, a three floor garage with stuff. Walls needed
to be demolished, fence, it was a danger for kids.
Judge ruled I have ten weeks to clean the house or go
to jail. Me. Stuff was his stuff. Expected me to do all
this when it was his stuff. I was responsible for his
stuff. So chauvinistic pig. It was like I was on the 14th
century. I was so surprised I didn't see any guillotines
to decapitate women if they said no.

(A deafening buzz overtakes the music.)

(April)

(MONDO joins DR HULL.)

DR HULL: What's this?

MONDO: My patch.

DR HULL: Something happen?

MONDO: Didn't you get my call?

DR HULL: Yes, you said the pain was getting worse. That's not unusual.

MONDO: It was not unusual, it was unbearable, so I finally tried this patch.

DR HULL: How'd you get that idea?

MONDO: Well, I do have some ideas.

DR HULL: It help?

MONDO: My headache went away.

DR HULL: That's interesting. It makes sense. You're blocking the source of the conflict.

MONDO: You mean to tell me you have a Ph.D on eyes and it never occurred to you I could use an eye patch? *(Pause)* Did you hear me?

DR HULL: I was listening. You found something that helps. That's good.

MONDO: It helps me sleep, but that's the top of the iceberg. *(Pause)* It creates other problems. After a few hours, I feel like I'm getting high. Everything looks different.

DR HULL: How?

MONDO: Things keep changing where they are. For example, I have a chair in my living room, it's out in the middle of the room. And next to that, a coffee table with a vase of branches, and behind that, a sofa. Well, all this, the whole room, could have been some kind of wallpaper. It was all completely flat. Like when I walked into the room all the furniture jumped into the wall. It was an empty room with a very detailed wallpaper.

DR HULL: Using only one eye is a big adjustment. There's no depth. Throws off your judgment. You can't tell how far away things are. How close they're getting. Be careful going down stairs.

MONDO: So either I wear the patch and see like this, or have the headaches?

DR HULL: Essentially, those are your options, yes.

MONDO: Oh great. I'm between a rock and hell.

DR HULL: Up to you.

MONDO: There is no choice there. I know I'm supposed to reduce my stress, but it raises my stress to know I have to reduce my stress! That's why stress is the silent killer of women, stress-related heart attack, stress-related stroke, stress-related kids, a trip to the store, even my flowers look under a lot of stress!

(DR HULL *places the cymbal before* MONDO, *and hands her the makeshift drumstick.*)

MONDO: What is this?

DR HULL: You're angry. Sometimes, you get mad, you wanna hit something. I think the cymbal's good.

MONDO: This is ridiculous. Last night, I have this pain, I die for! (*At a loss for words, she hits the cymbal.*) I was all night, on bed, I didn't close my eyes, didn't went to sleep, nothing. I put a cold compact, it made no difference. I stayed all night without sleep. (*Hits cymbal*) I wanted to take a pill, but I didn't know what to take. Tylenol, and all this off-the-counter drugs, if you overdose once you need a liver transplant. (*Hits cymbal*) This is bullshit!

(MONDO *hits the cymbal two more times and goes on to take a few swings at* DR HULL; *he takes the stick and cymbal away.*)

DR HULL: Have you been listening to the pieces I recommended?

MONDO: I went to the symphony. It didn't help me. How many weeks I'm coming here and nothing changes?

DR HULL: It won't happen overnight. It's a process.

MONDO: It's a torture for me.

DR HULL: What's torture?

MONDO: The music.

DR HULL: How is that torture?

MONDO: I don't hear the way I used to hear. *(Pause)* I used to hear and I cry, but I cry from euphoria. Acoustic building, oh gosh, I was my heart there, I felt my heart there. Now it doesn't sound music. It sounds when I pound a chicken for Chicken Kiev. Just bom, bom, bom. Then ZZZZ. I had my ears checked and told me nothing is wrong.

DR HULL: That's interesting. You know, rare cases can start to affect other senses. *(Pause)* I think the music's helping you. As a matter of fact, I recommend you move beyond listening to actual playing. *(Pause)* You have a piano?

MONDO: I have, but is very old. Somebody gave it to my husband. It doesn't tune.

DR HULL: Doesn't matter.

MONDO: I don't know any songs.

DR HULL: Even better. Improvise. It's about what you feel. No matter how bad you think it sounds. It deserves to be heard.

(MONDO *carries her chair to the piano. She lifts the keyguard.)*

MONDO: I took classical piano in Greece. A hundred years ago. *(Pause)* It wasn't anything, it wasn't suppose to be anything, I was a female, I was suppose to be getting ready to give five births. *(Pause)* I always wanted to learn a whole piece. Like la la la la nana na. The Piraeus song. Learn something like that to play it somewhere. I liked Beethoven and Mozart. They have written so many pieces. People who really know music, you say Mozart is not enough. They want to know *No. 5, No. 3.* The exactly piece. But I never learned anything, it was all theory. To read music. The different scales. The different, to play the E sounds. The C sound. When you hear music to know what it is. *(She tests a few keys, each one more toneless than the next.)* Oh my god, they're all dead. *(She tries to run through a scale.)* Do sa li ray mi do. La la la la la. Do ray me fo la si do. Black adds some accent. *(She tries to incorporate the black keys.)* Do rah do rah do rah mi.

(Beautiful piano tones from a C D fill the room. She positions her hands.)

MONDO: One hand plays the bass. The other hand plays the details. *(She practices mimicking a sequence from the C D.)* One hand, just bass. Other hand does all the work. *(Awkwardly, she tries to coordinate her hands, but the song quickly begins to lose any sense of melody. It unfolds continuously in a torrent of toneless plinking, with an unpleasant rattling reverberation, sounding much more like an ice pick on a snare drum than Bach. She plays with increasing intensity until she drowns out the recording entirely and we hear nothing but noise. Suddenly, she slams the keyguard closed. She carries her chair back to DR HULL.)*

(May)

(DR HULL scoots his chair very close to MONDO's.)

DR HULL: Look over my shoulder, stare wide, and blink normally.

MONDO: O K.

(MONDO's *eyes remain fixed on a target.* DR HULL *holds the lens close to her eye, and realizes her eye patch is still on.)*

DR HULL: Oops. *(He removes the patch, and tilts the lens in different directions, resting his hand on her head for steadiness.)*

MONDO: Are the—

DR HULL: Hold still. *(As he continues the exam, he drops the lens.)* Oh for Christsake. *(He picks it up, and finishes the exam.)* Thank you.

MONDO: So what happened?

DR HULL: Well, I'd like to see it going down more. The sacks were starting to shrink, but they're filling back up again.

MONDO: I'm going into circles.

DR HULL: It sometimes happens in prolonged cases. Yours is one of the most extreme I've ever seen. *(Pause)* Would you be able to come in again tomorrow?

MONDO: Tomorrow? Tomorrow. If I had a voice, I'd start singing.

DR HULL: Are you available? I'd like to incorporate GIM sessions into your treatment.

MONDO: What is that?

DR HULL: Guided Imagery and Music. You listen to music in a relaxed state, and I talk to you. It gives us a way to go places we can't go in normal conversation. *(Pause)* I'm available after three.

MONDO: I can only come in the morning.

DR HULL: That's fine. I had a cancellation.

MONDO: When?

DR HULL: What?

MONDO: What time was the cancellation?

DR HULL: Oh, it was. Lemme see. *(He takes his Blackberry off his belt, and goes through the motions of scrolling through an empty calendar)* What time could you come?

MONDO: Nine.

DR HULL: Perfect. See you then.

(MONDO walks slowly across the stage, toward the piano.)

MONDO: He didn't discriminate against junk. Driving around sees plastic, he picks it up. How much junk, you can't imagine, folks. Sees a plastic flower on the street, he picks it up. He wanted me to put a "Baby on Board" in my car because he picked it up somewhere! I don't have a baby! He had this mentality of people who are alcoholic. Driving, next block, there is trash there, he takes it. He saw something, he said, this is brand new. He picked up computers. Going here and there to find stuff, in case he needs. Everything and anything and everywhere! "I can use this to make business." He was gonna fix it and sell it. He never sold a thing. *(Pause)* First time I realized how junky he was: I came to his house. Car was junky, he said how good car was. He has this junk car, big car full of painting. I said what are you gonna do with all this? He said, "We just got house, we can use painting." Right. "I bought all this for nothing, only a hundred dollars." We had to carry it to the house, two gallons, one gallon, all day carrying the painting. So much painting, we could paint the whole neighborhood, folks! We gave some to a couple friends, they brought it back, said it was no good. That's why the store was giving it away, it was no good! Where can you use this stuff? *(Pause)* We had a friend in Philly who worked next to the river and a flood took his car. He was going to give away his car for free. We call the guy, my husband starts asking

questions, "What's the problem with the car?" He goes
on, problems, problems, the car didn't work! "Does the
door open?" "No." "Does the window open?" "No."
"Can you turn it on?" "No." He kept asking questions.
Nothing you could say would make him not want this
car! Can't put on A/C cause the car stinks. He says,
"Maybe I can take it to a place, and I can clean it." He
had to have that car. Like he had to have everything.
(Pause) Betrayal means shit. Betrayal means you were
an idiot and you feel sorry for yourself. Forget the
word betrayal. There was no betrayal, he was just
doing what he always did, collecting. Of course he
would pick up a girlfriend, he picked up everything.
You can never have enough junk, folks.

(DR HULL *speaks from the back wall.*)

DR HULL: My back is hurting a lot lately. I'm not
wallowing in self-pity, but I do have terrible strange
pains in the middle of the night.
I have a pain the size of a fist burning and pushing
into my rib cage. I ran some hot shower-hose water all
over my back. It wasn't enough. I rubbed on Miracle
Ice, it didn't help, and I couldn't get the smell off me. I
spent five hours at Saint Joe's. They X-rayed my chest.
Not my back where the pain is. The radiology nurses
tossed me around like a bean bag on those steel X-ray
tables. I can tell they think I'm making it up, so I'm
back to the painful drawing board. Something weird is
wrong with me. Physician heal thyself. That's me. I've
got to get better by myself somehow. This morning I
managed to get downstairs without screaming.

(June)

(DR HULL *remains near the back wall. The glare of light
softens to a soothing blue. Classical music starts to play as*
MONDO *sits down and puts her feet up.*)

DR HULL: Do you see anything in your mind when you hear this?

MONDO: With this music, I can see, angels dancing over my head. Or women. *(Responding to a change in the music:)* Or here is an angel with a trumpet. Somehow this music would be appropriate for angels to dance. *(The music changes again.)* Some evil tries to distract the angels from playing soft music. Evil coming through the dance, breaking and separating them like a storm. Angels with wings and evil had horns and tails. Angels run around in a triangle, lose track of each other. I don't know who wins in the end.

DR HULL: Where are you?

MONDO: I'm in a field.

DR HULL: What kind of field?

MONDO: A big, acres and acres of land. Full of spring flowers, summer flowers. Wildflowers. You can pick as many as you can, and they charge you very little. Wildflowers they're not to pick actually, they're to be left alone. Like ornaments of the field because they don't last if you pick them. Next day they're dead. Flowers from flower shops, they're not real. I mean, they're real, but they're controlled by human beings. By people who control their height, their weight, their color, their supplements. They make the flower do something it would not naturally do.

DR HULL: What color is the field?

MONDO: Lots of yellow, purple, orange. Zinnias, my favorite flowers, Zinions, bright red, yellow, purple. Very bright. Those colors in South America, aren't they? Mexico. Very bright.

DR HULL: Are you picking flowers?

MONDO: Yes. Sunflowers. Because they're big and bulky. The Zinnias, usually when you find Zinnias, they're very short.

DR HULL: What do the sunflowers look like?

MONDO: Oh, are big sunflowers, with the center, big, black and shiny. So shiny. Looks like cellophane. The leaves are nice and long, and yellow, the petals. So I cut them with a knife, diagonally so it has a big opening at the end of the stem, so it absorbs a lot of water, and I put it in a vase.

(The music changes. Some buzzing is audible.)

DR HULL: You've left the field?

MONDO: I have to get ready. People are coming for a wine tasting party. Right now flies are starting to show up.

DR HULL: Where?

MONDO: The living room. They're walking around. I thought they were coming from the opening door, I'm looking for a crack in the window. These flies are big. And shiny. I'm trying to get rid of them, with a towel, open the basement door, get them in the basement. I don't know where they're coming from, it's horrendous, I can't keep up with them, I don't want them to sit on any food. I'm trying to open a window. Is too heavy.

DR HULL: Is anyone there with you?

MONDO: My husband.

DR HULL: What do you want to say to him?

MONDO: Help me.

DR HULL: Is he helping you?

MONDO: He's gone.

DR HULL: Can you open the window yourself?

MONDO: The windows of this house don't open. The ropes that control them are broken.

DR HULL: Can you prop one open?

MONDO: I need a piece of wood. Oh gosh. Oh goodness. I know where the flies came. The warmth of the room released them off the center of the flowers. They came from the sunflowers. I brought them into my house.

DR HULL: What are you doing now?

(The music changes.)

MONDO: I have that plastic paper with gooey gum, they unroll, they are like spiral, yellow strips.

DR HULL: Are they working?

MONDO: One of them got stuck on my hair. Oh boy. The flies are coming now. They're in my hair. They're in my hair!

(Buzzing becomes louder)

MONDO: All I hear is ZZZZZZZ. ZZZZZZZ!

DR HULL: Should I turn off the music?

MONDO: Stop the music. Stop, stop it!

(Silence. The light intensifies to its normal color and brightness. MONDO walks to the piano. DR HULL turns to the audience.)

DR HULL: Oh I dread this time of day. These young future presidents, doctors, lawyers, and hopheads that are leaving school with boomboxed cars. I shudder wondering how summer is gonna be. *(Pause)* I can't believe how downhill Reading has become. All the old timers died or moved away. They were replaced by kids with babies, the mothers are sixteen, pushing strollers and pregnant. They're out on their porches, their little children on their cigarette-smoking laps.

It was raining and a guy came out in a T-shirt with
shampoo on his head. Washing his hair in the rain.
Every day I think I see the cheapest, ugliest tattoo,
but then I see the next one. L-O-Y-L-T-Y. Why would
you get a loyalty tattoo on your back and misspelled?
(Pause) I am so uncomfortable. I feel like I'm made
of rubber and mush for brains. I didn't do anything
today except put a frozen clam pie in the oven. If I get
hungry, I'll be O K. I won't take another dose until
tomorrow. I'm completely useless. Now I must write
checks.

(MONDO *speaks from the piano.*)

MONDO: I'm thinking moving back to Greece, folks.
Our Greek Romeo and Juliet jumped off the Parthenon.
When things get bad, I'll go to the Acropolis and jump
off the Parthenon. *(Pause)* I took it all for granted when
I had it. I thought I would have it forever. I didn't
notice it. There is summer, there is a moon there on
your balcony. Mountains across you can touch. A
mountain, the ocean, a show of lightning. The wildlife.
Olive oil trees. Nature is. Little wave. Blue water, the
white afro of the wave. Nature is amazing. This blue
water is out of the world. Turkwoz blue, you just
swim. You're not afraid, you just swim. Not these
endless beaches here. Here you go to the beaches and
there is no end. *(Pause)* Patras, where I'm from, is
gonna be the art center of Europe because of all the
work they did for the Olympics. Incredible French
bridge, it's a masterpiece. Everything is hanging in the
air. Square plaza who is historical. Thanks they kept
some neoclassic architecture. Theater which worth it
to go, no microphones and five thousand people, open
air. The theaters here are ugly. Four walls, I cannot take
them. We're prisoners here. The hell of the life. Tell me
again why I'm in this ugly city.

(July)

(MONDO *carries her chair back to* DR HULL. *He appears to be steadying himself by gripping the back of his own chair.*)

MONDO: It's not getting better?

DR HULL: I'm fine. I was just dizzy for a second.

MONDO: I was talking about my eye.

DR HULL: Of course. We'll look at that in a minute. *(Pause)* Have you been taking it easy?

MONDO: No, the Judge would not allow it.

DR HULL: The Judge.

MONDO: Yes, he listened to my husband's lawyer. Max something, three other names after that. He knew the inside story, he knew the outside story, he knew all the stories, and he made a story out of my words. So they ordered me to clean my husband's other house. This is what I'm doing the past two weeks, ten hours a day, and I didn't even get to the escape steps outside. They're piled with junk all the way up the side of the building, and they're full of rust. I need to wear a safety hat to go there.

DR HULL: The Judge ordered you to clean your husband's house?

MONDO: Yes.

DR HULL: That's odd. What did your attorney say?

MONDO: I didn't have. I had to present myself.

DR HULL: You should have an attorney.

MONDO: Yes.

DR HULL: What happened with your house?

MONDO: I got to keep it.

DR HULL: Good.

MONDO: Yes, wonderful. Well, he lied that's why.

(Pause)

DR HULL: You know, I know somebody. He was in my
class in medical school. Got kicked out for cheating.
He's a lawyer now. I can call him, if you want.

MONDO: Why?

DR HULL: Because you need a lawyer.

MONDO: Oh, no, I don't, I don't, I don't.

DR HULL: I think you do.

MONDO: I can't afford it.

DR HULL: Don't worry. He's a good guy. I'll call him
right now. *(He stands up and takes his Blackberry off his
belt.)* If I can work this. I keep taking pictures of my ear.

MONDO: You don't have to.

(DR HULL dials and places the Blackberry to his ear. Pause)

DR HULL: John Stoltzfus, please. This is Lou Hull. *(Long
pause)* Hey, John. Yeah, how are ya? I'm calling because
I wanna refer a client to you. Her name is Mondo. This
is someone in dire need, and very deserving. I told
her you're the best. Yeah, yeah. Actually, I wondered
if you could give her a break financially. You do pro-
bono work don't you? I thought… Uh-huh. O K. You
don't have to take that tone. I can't even ask you a
question? Yeah? Well, fuck you, John! Right. Go fuck
yourself! *(He hangs up and returns to* MONDO.*)* Turns out
he's too busy right now.

MONDO: Sure.

DR HULL: Sorry about that.

MONDO: That's O K. I appreciate it. I appreciate your
offer. Was very kind. Really was.

DR HULL: Rest your head. *(Pause)* Just look straight up.
Keep your focus right there. *(Positioning his handheld
lens over her eye)* I'm just gonna open your eye. You'll
feel some pressure. *(Retracting her eyelids, while holding*

the lens directly over her left eye) That's good. Just keep looking up. Perfect. *(He raises the lens slightly higher, resting his fingers on her cheek and forehead. One of his hands pushes some of her hair back, then absently begins to pet her hair.)* Does your hair just naturally do this?

MONDO: Pardon?

DR HULL: Beautiful. So soft.

(MONDO reaches up and removes DR HULL's hand from her hair, replacing it with her own.)

MONDO: I can hold it back.

DR HULL: You're tough, Diamondo. You'd never guess it by looking at you. You're a little thing, you have your fingernails painted. They don't fool me, you could cut glass with those things.

(DR HULL repositions the lens. His fingers linger a moment too long on MONDO's cheek. He leans uncomfortably close to her face, appearing to smell her neck. She is frozen.)

MONDO: Is something wrong?

(DR HULL moves the lens to a different angle.)

DR HULL: Almost done.

(DR HULL's face drifts closer to her neck in a sleepy attempt at a kiss. MONDO stands up.)

DR HULL: O K!

MONDO: What happened?

DR HULL: Just getting a closer look.

MONDO: Am I on the track?

DR HULL: At six months. I would like to see more progress by now.If it goes on much longer, it'll lead to retinal atrophy. *(Pause)* If we need to get more aggressive with it, we will. We'll know in a few weeks.

(MONDO walks toward the piano.)

DR HULL: I fell asleep trying to eat creamed ham, big whoop. I told you I was half-awake when I sat down, but you go on and on: "I just got a perm, my neighbor said, 'Oh, it's beautiful, one curl on top of another.' And I said, 'Yes,' and she said, 'Yes.' And I told her its curls are tight because I didn't comb my hair, and she said, 'Oh,' and I said, 'Yes.'" How many times did you tell me the hairdresser got scissor-happy? I know you're not senile, but you tell me the same thing over and over. I don't have the patience. And if you're gonna insist that I come downstairs and have supper with you, after I told you I wasn't feeling right, then don't be surprised when I pass out at the table. I was in bed till three, I felt lousy, I wasn't hungry, I'm lucky I didn't fall on my face. *(Pause)* Yes, Ma, I will hang your planters tomorrow.

(MONDO speaks from the piano.)

MONDO: Crap, folks. I didn't wanna cry in front of him, but lately I'm the crying baby. I'm crying, I never pretend I live to the fullest. I got something from my mom that's difficult to inherit. Not money. To be brave. Spirit. Never my parents say the most important thing is to be happy. Say, when I got married, say: you no longer exist. *(Pause)* Most females embedded in society we invest so much in the relationship. Even the high-educated, high-intelligent women. I know people change, grow, not always the direction you like. And men fool around. They love you. But they love ten other women. *(Pause)* My friend Melpomeni found Yianni Malakas on the computer and said, "O-M-G-O-D". She moved to Oregon for his job. She wasn't doing anything of substance. That becomes baby and husband. I wouldn't wanna be an ant in her shoes. She's the only one I could stand from the Greek community. As the bell rings seven o'clock they're in church. Say all crap about God, I don't give a damn

about God. I don't need any freak around me to make
me feel edgy. Something happened to me, I called my
husband. I used to come home, ask how was your day.
Now come home and I am myself. Eat myself. Sleep
myself. Be alone. Something happens to me, I don't
call anybody. *(Pause)* I didn't like who my husband
changed into be, so I'm disappointed at him. But we
had chemistry. We are so differently intellectually and
life orientation, but we had chemistry, and I could
have tried. I rushed to the divorce and now all the
good times are dead. It hits you. It might hit you the
day, or tomorrow but when it comes, it's such a tear-
jerking shit. *(Pause)* My husband was part of my Greek
identity. Now my Greek period is over. I need to lose
some part of my character, what I carry culturally. It
has to be, everything has been destroyed for me as far
as Greek. I need to integrate, involve more. Embrace
more America. *(Pause)* I brought all my books to study.
I have a self-helper, a good self-helper book. It helps
yourself.

(August)

(MONDO *joins* DR HULL *who is seated in front of the
cymbal.)*

MONDO: I found a lawyer. *(Pause)* Greek guy. Nick
Papas. Through the church. At least the church is good
for something. *(Pause)* Very good. Very knowledgable
man. He's very nice, maintains a yoga nature. Always
a positive advice. *(Pause)* I want to thank you. You
inspired me to look for him. I would bring you a big
plate of baklava, but I'm recovering housewife, can't
cook.

DR HULL: This isn't good. There are subretinal
lipofucinoid flecks on your peripheral fundus.

MONDO: Oh my gosh.

DR HULL: Don't panic.

MONDO: *(Panicked)* Why!

DR HULL: I'd like to get a date for you at the Vitreous Retina Macula Center for laser treatment.

MONDO: The surgery?

DR HULL: Yes.

MONDO: But you said, I'm too young for that.

DR HULL: I said I would only consider it as a last resort.

MONDO: You said it's too risky!

DR HULL: Look, I feel for you—

MONDO: Why don't you have the surgery if you feel so much for me!

DR HULL: We're calm. Deep breath. *(Taking a deep breath)*

MONDO: If I have it now, what happens when I'm seventy?

DR HULL: No one can say for sure.

MONDO: I can! Everything falls apart. It doesn't last, you said—

DR HULL: Not necessarily—

MONDO: I'm not interested in hanging in the air! It's not a good feeling!

DR HULL: What will happen in the long term is unknown, yes. There're risks. But we have to weigh them against the chances of permanent visual loss. And I don't like those chances right now.

MONDO: *(In tears)* I create this. I'm too much attached. *(Pause)* I know I need to move on, I want to go another rite of passage, turn over a new page in my life. You need to take your life your hands. You need to stand for yourself. I can't. Some people next day, they can turn a page and they're over. Pass threshold, different

door, different life. I'm not able to do this. I carry a
lot of baggage on my shoulder. Whenever you're
disappointed, it's cause your attachment. I am so much
attached. I know this. I carry all this. Someone said
something five years ago. Oh crap. I don't know how
to live at the moment. I'm not able to over this stage
and phase, and I want to be over.

DR HULL: You didn't do anything wrong. We've just
exhausted all the alternatives. The eye can only take so
much. (Pause) You don't have to make a decision right
now, but it can't wait more than a month. And I would
strongly advise you to have the surgery.

(Classical music starts to play. MONDO begins a slow walk
towards the piano, via the back wall.)

MONDO: Walking home with one eye, the street is a
bootcamp course. All kinds of things in your way.
Including people. If they're on this side, I can't see
them till I'm stepping on them. Thanks it started to
rain, it covered my crying. It's raining chair legs, that
my mother called it. I was wearing these healthy shoes
that a guy on the Italian mountains made. They're
so hard, they just make your feet tired. And all the
water was in my toes, the shoe was like a leather bag,
it wouldn't let anything out. (Pause) In the house, I
had to wash my hands and I was looking at the sink.
I couldn't think how to touch the faucet to turn it. I
never thought before, how do I turn the faucet? But
looking at it, at that moment, there was nothing to
grab, so I didn't know how I was gonna turn the damn
thing. Finally, I just closed my eyes and felt for it. With
both eyes closed, I could feel a part of something.
Only with my eyes closed. I felt like I could see better
closing my eyes. I could see what I remembered, and
I could feel the rest. Most of the time that's what I did.
I just closed my eyes and pretty soon, I felt like I was
part of the world again. But the world was black, so

that became my world. The rest was somebody else's pictures.

(DR HULL *speaks from his seat by the cymbal.*)

DR HULL: Even with my head fuzzed my abilities haven't wavered. I can still think clearly. When you don't pay attention, you make dumb mistakes. That's a problem. But I'm alert when I need to be. I remember every detail from what I just watched. I have a photographic mind. It was called The Pacific Salmon. They have this homing device. Every year they go back to where they were born. They swim upstream. They're just muscle. They have to go upstream, up these waterfalls, there are thousands of them, they shoot out of the water, and bears are waiting there biting the air. *(Pause)* They have mercury in their brains magnetized to the earth that tells them when they're home. Sometimes with no rain, the rivers dry up, and they get stuck. Bears just pick them out of the dry riverbed. Then they lay their eggs and die. Their skeletons fertilize the forest with salt minerals. *(Pause)* It's amazing thousands of years of evolution propel them to their death.

(MONDO *is now seated at her piano.*)

MONDO: Don't ever get sunflowers into your house. They're nice but they're full of flies. You can't see them, they dig their little heads so deep into the flower, you only see the shiny surface. *(Hitting random keys)* But that's flies. It's all flies. It's disgusting. The damn flies! What's the matter with it? *(Pounding the keys)* Get out! Damn these flies! *(Pound)* Damn flies get to hell out of here! *(Pound)* Get goddamnit! *(Pound)* Out! Get OOOOOOUUUUUT! *(Pound)*

(MONDO's *last pound is more than the piano can take, and something snaps inside. We hear the rattling reverberations of whatever broke as the lights go black.* DR HULL *stands in the darkness and illuminates his face with his pen-light.)*

DR HULL: I've had it with Tom Sawyer's Diner. I went in there one day, I walked in the kitchen, looking for the bathroom. Hair flying all over, no hair net, nothing, haven't shaved in god knows when, food all over the floor. I got a hot roast beef sandwich, mashed potatoes, beans outta the can, and a long lady looking thing, a daddy long legs spider was on the plate. I said to the waitress, "Would you eat that?" She got sick and threw up. They gave me the meal for nothing, but how could I ever go back? *(Pause)* Now when I go out, I make a habit of walking into the kitchen. If it's filthy, I'm gone. And I don't care how good the food is, I won't wait more than twenty minutes.

(September)

*(*MONDO *joins* DR HULL *in the dark and sits down. As he directs his pen-light to her left eye, the shadow of her head fills the wall.)*

DR HULL: I'll be damned.

MONDO: What.

DR HULL: That spot used to be verging on the optic nerve, all the way over here. And the other one. I can barely make it out anymore.

MONDO: They shrank?

DR HULL: Considerably.

MONDO: So I won't need to have the surgery?

DR HULL: Not if this continues.

MONDO: My gosh. Thanks to you.

DR HULL: Sometimes it happens spontaneously. It can't be explained. I don't think I had anything to do with it.

(Full lights come on.)

MONDO: Yes, was the music. That's what did it. I know. When I broke my piano.

DR HULL: You broke your piano?

MONDO: Well, all the time my neck is like an octopus is squeezing the hell out of me, all this tension. But after that, is gone. Was such relief.

DR HULL: How did you break it?

MONDO: I was trying to play a song. With baseball bats. The way I was playing was so hard, was like I had baseball bats in my hands, but was a blast. Pretty soon, it went "booooong" and that was it. No more sounds were coming out of it. It had enough of that. *(Pause)* Somehow, after that happened, I didn't hear it anymore. The ZZZZZ. My hearing is back into normal gear.

(A buzzing sound. It's DR HULL's Blackberry. He takes it off his belt and throws it across the room. It crashes loudly offstage.)

MONDO: Is that how you answer your phone?

DR HULL: I don't know how to turn it off. I hope I just broke it.

(MONDO reads an unseen eye chart.)

MONDO: Three, five, six.

DR HULL: Are you going in order?

MONDO: Now wait a minute. Five, six, three.

DR HULL: That's better. Anything smaller?

MONDO: Uh. S—. Seven.

DR HULL: A little bit of a struggle.

MONDO: A little, yes. But I noticed I could read. For about seven months I was page four, now I'm a hundred.

DR HULL: What have you been reading?

MONDO: Oh. Van Gogh.

DR HULL: Van Gogh?

MONDO: Yes.

DR HULL: What did he write?

MONDO: Letters. I want to learn how to write letters.

DR HULL: Are you sure you want to learn from him?

MONDO: Why not?

DR HULL: He was nuts.

MONDO: Well, I saw some thank you letters in there
and I have a hard time writing thank you letters.
(Pause) It's good to read something. It's, I want to build
the skill. You stretch, first of all, the brain, learning new
words. I have vocabulary books, the dictionary. I need
to improve my English.

DR HULL: Your English is fine. Once you get used to it.
(Pause) Any undulation in the field of vision?

MONDO: Like a wavy thing? No waviness. And the
dimness is much less.

DR HULL: That's great. Your retina is regenerating.
How are things otherwise? Are you divorced yet?

MONDO: We're to a standstill until the next hearing.
He's asking for alimony. He says he hurt his back, he
can't work. Of course, it's lies, he's a deadbeef. It's
all games, very playful games. I mean who is gonna
throw stones to who? *(Pause)* I'm not getting excited,
I'm gonna declare innocent. Nick pulled me on the
side and told me they'll throw it out because he has
no documentation. *(Pause)* Believe it or not, he called
me. *(Pause)* Just to strike conversation, he tells me he
wants me back. The scum of the dirt. He sounded so
sweet and nice over the phone, he told me stories, you

know men how they stories. How he loves me, how he was tired baby-sitting her kids. He told me everything, how she needed him so much he couldn't drive with both hands on the wheel, she had to hold one. Listen now, he tells me maybe if I was treating him different, he would have stayed with me. If I was treating him different. A lot of chips on his shoulders. Said with me, I am the way I am. With her, she is the way she is. Between the two, we don't meet his needs. He wanted both of us! Can you believe? Funny, I can see at all after that. I'm not sure my pupils are still in the center of my eyeballs. *(Pause)* I told him he can be an Arab, he can have twenty wives, but all I can offer is slapping him left and right. *(Pause)* Next day he came and stole my jewelry. *(Pause)* The jewelry he gave me, he took to give to her. I wasn't home, he broke my house. He had key. He took everything. I changed the locks right away.

DR HULL: Did you call the cops?

MONDO: No.

DR HULL: You don't want to press charges?

MONDO: My next neighbors didn't see anything, I asked them, and the other side neighbor, the architect, nobody saw him.

DR HULL: You should at least file a report.

MONDO: That's O K.

DR HULL: Why not?

MONDO: I don't want to ridikill myself, have a record that this happened.

DR HULL: Are you afraid of him?

MONDO: I'm not afraid, he's an idiot. Today I regret. That's the only feeling. Regret. *(Pause)* Imagine now. I loved this man. And the feeling, you were with someone, and you lived everyday and now they do all this stuff, trying to cheat you. *(Getting choked up)* Oh boy. Oh goodness. It's the thing that never leaves.

DR HULL: If anything else happens with your husband, have the bastard arrested. *(Pause)* He needs to be taught a lesson. Better the police, than me. Though if you want me to, I'll go to his house and brandish some eye drops.

(MONDO almost laughs.)

DR HULL: If anything'll set him straight, it's tobramycin ophthalmic suspension.

MONDO: That's O K.

DR HULL: Suit yourself.

MONDO: Smooth riding from here?

(DR HULL is unsure what she means)

MONDO: *(With gesture)* Smooth riding?

DR HULL: Oh sure, you could say that.

(MONDO walks back to the piano. DR HULL turns toward the audience.)

DR HULL: Where's Socks? Socks! You want your mouse? Get it! Get it! Get it! YOU GOT IT! You GOT that RED DOT! *(Crouching down)* What's amatter, Socksy? You didn't finish your ice cream. Did you see the paper? Look at that. Know who that is? That's Greg from the Medicine Shoppe. When I walked in, he started shaking a no-no finger at me. Refused to fill my script. Well, he had a vascular incident in his neck. *(To the obituary)* Now you're dead, and I am not. So screw you. Congrats, Greg. Asshole.

(October)

(MONDO crosses to meet DR HULL.)

MONDO: Dr. Hull.

DR HULL: Hi, Mondo.

MONDO: What did you say to Doreen?

DR HULL: I don't know what you're talking about.

MONDO: She said I didn't owe anything.

DR HULL: That's interesting.

MONDO: You erased the bill.

DR HULL: I wouldn't know how to do that. I'm a doctor. I treat patients. I wasn't trained to handle the administrative part.

MONDO: Then how do you explain it?

DR HULL: I don't know. Ask my mother.

MONDO: Your mother?

DR HULL: Yes, my mother, Doreen.

MONDO: You talked to her!

DR HULL: I talk to her all the time, she's my ma.

MONDO: What did you say?

DR HULL: I just said there was a dispute about your bill and she did the rest.

MONDO: I knew it. I knew you did this. You didn't have to do that. Doesn't that create a problem for you?

DR HULL: The truth is, working with you has been a unique opportunity for me. Consider it my thanks to you.

(Pause)

MONDO: Dr. Hull.

DR HULL: Yes?

MONDO: Do you know what a crescent moon is?

DR HULL: A crescent moon?

MONDO: Do you know what it looks like?

DR HULL: Of course.

MONDO: Well, I've been watching the Foods Network, and I would like to make you a crescent moon for dinner. *(Pause)* Really, I never thought I would have an opinion for cooking again. All those years I did what I was suppose to do, got up, do beans, coffee from beans, orange juice with hands, I thought if you ever see me in the kitchen again, don't hold your breath! But this is different now. I was watching this food melt like butter in front of me and I thought, I would like to make this and taste this. And I would like to share this with you.

DR HULL: That's not necessary.

MONDO: I know, I want to.

DR HULL: You don't want to make me dinner.

MONDO: I do.

DR HULL: Well, I haven't had much of an appetite lately. *(Pause)* Thank you for your invitation. I never had a crescent moon for dinner.

MONDO: That's the dessert.

DR HULL: Enjoy your dessert.

(MONDO *leaves with her chair. She positions it flush against the back wall, and sits.*)

DR HULL: The last time I was in the paper I was nine years old holding a snake. I was interviewed for three hours. "Their bite doesn't hurt. To pick them up, you sit close to them and let them crawl up your arm. Don't let them dangle, they need their bodies supported all the time. And don't squeeze them. I like snakes because when they swallow a mouse whole you can watch the lump going down." *(Pause)* I feel pretty good except that I am sorta lifeless. Thank god for T V.

(November)

(DR HULL *places his chair flush against the back wall, directly across from* MONDO, *and sits facing her, as if in the booth of a diner.*)

DR HULL: Thank you for meeting me here.

MONDO: Of course. How are you?

DR HULL: Have you read what they're saying about me? *(Pause)* It's all lies. They didn't like that I wore rubber gloves when I treated people. They think I'm a quack cause I use music. They target me like a dartboard. They make all these accusations and the dominoes start to fall. I will not continue to be the main dartboard. It's not illegal to have arthritis. I have a form of chronic arthritis in my back. I didn't write phony prescriptions for myself. Why would I? I have an orthopedic surgeon. He gave me a hundred and eighty tablets in a little jar, basically a high level Advil, it worked perfect, but it was strong. It made me groggy. People got the worst impression. They raided my office, hey, this is missing, that's missing. That mean I took it? I have patients!

MONDO: I didn't know you were working at nursing homes.

DR HULL: Those nurses parked in my spot every day. The head nurse never said a word. She stood there smoking. "Hey bitch, why don't you smoke another one?" That's what I wanted to say to her. "That fat lady just took my spot, now I'm late." They didn't give a shit. They have done lethal harm in an act of pure spite. *(Pause)* I don't want them to take me away from Socks. I have nightmares about it. I have seconds to say goodbye. The A S P C A will kill her. *(Pause)* She's such an unusual cat. I pick her up by the tail and she loves it. It gets her spine in alignment. She grabs onto the carpet and looks up at you going nuts. *(Pause)* Socks is in her old age. I am very aware of how bad she smells when she poops, but I can't leave her now. When she makes her mistakes, I stay on top of it. Most people would have gotten rid of such a messy cat.

MONDO: Is there anything I can do?

DR HULL: My lawyer thinks that it would help to have some letters of support, defending me.

MONDO: Oh gosh. I'm happy with the way things turned. I'll tell this to the lawyers, the Judges, everybody. I'm still recommending you to my co-workers. Has my boss come to see you?

DR HULL: No one has come to see me. I had to surrender my license until the court rules.

MONDO: O K, O K.

DR HULL: Thank you, Mondo.

(MONDO *gets up, places her chair just off the edge of the plywood floor and disappears behind the wall.*)

DR HULL: Maybe I should visit my cousin in Frisco. Always coolish. Wind off the water. Ride the trolly, what a thrill. Especially if you sit in front. It can't stop. Locks in a rail, smell 'em burn, it's wood, hanging on the side, that's O K. People bringing apples for fare. Turn the car around it starts back up again like a turn table.

(*Mid-sentence, the plywood wall lifts to reveal the vast house of the actual theater, with the plywood floor extending over the first few rows, and* MONDO *perched at its edge, seemingly floating above the plush velvet seats.* DR HULL *places his chair just off the lip of the plywood floor and exits. She stands alone in this world of lush dimension, full of depth and richness. Wood molding blooms from the ceiling. A curved balcony juts over the orchestra. Exuberant bursts of light dangle from chandeliers. Radiant, she faces the audience, some of whom may just be realizing they've been seated on stage the whole time.*)

(Classical music starts to play.)

MONDO: The symphony is perfect for me. To be with
people away from everything. Two hours have to sit
still. Time goes so fast, don't become fidgety. It's an
education. Learn about the organs and how everything
connects on stage. How they connect. When it's time
for the violin to connect with the piano and the oboe.
It's amazing how many organs are on stage. How they
interwind, with one, with the other, and create this
melody, this music. *(Pause)* If they were by themselves,
there's a monotony. If it's just one violin, I can't listen.
The sound annoys my hearing. Very high-pitched, I
can't stand it. But you have a violin, then add a bass,
that makes it more harmonious, more exciting, how
they connect. Where they were weak, now they were
good. You can't hear the differences, can't hear the
wrong things. All those organs complement each other.
I watch their hands when they play the violin, they all
move the same way, all play the same song, otherwise
it's offbeat. Different ages, all different people, they
synchronize, like ballet, they do the same movement.
They're fascinating. *(Pause)* Watch one section: horns.
Watch one section: violinists. My eye goes to the
violinists, they move the most. They complement the
orchestra. Without them, you would miss that organ.

*(DR HULL enters a door in the back of the theater, and sits in
the last row.)*

MONDO: In front of me is a man and a woman, the who
and who of Reading, so I have to look through their
necks, between the two necks, that space where I can
see a hand moving while it's playing on that brown
piece of violin. How fast. Doesn't lift her wrist. It's
like something is crawling. This violinist, I can only
see her hand. Her hand looks like a spider. Very thin,
white, and very thin. Like a spider is making a nest.
Going up and down of the wood where the cords are.

Is that something? The people who wrote music, they included the violin. Without, it would be a void.

(The music gradually swells to a passionate orchestral uproar. MONDO *turns and descends the elevated platform. She walks toward the back of the house.)*

DR HULL: Mondo.

*(*MONDO *turns.)*

MONDO: You were behind me the whole time?

DR HULL: I came late. I didn't wanna disturb you.

*(*MONDO *sits. She and* DR HULL *are both in the last row, separated by a gulf of empty seats.)*

MONDO: So what did you think of the new one?

DR HULL: The new what?

MONDO: Conductor.

DR HULL: I didn't notice.

MONDO: I was on awe. He was fun. He's not stuffed. We needed someone like him to spice the whole thing. I don't know if the community will like him. They want to feel safe in their little cocoons and god forbid if anyone shakes them.

DR HULL: What happened to the old guy?

MONDO: He's gone.

DR HULL: Just like that?

MONDO: Well, every time he took his position, it was like, "Let's bring out the dead walking people." He might have a heart attack right there. Not only that, he had a problem with the orchestra and they hold a grunge against him. It's not good for people to live too long. They screw everything up. When your time is out you should leave. Show us your talent, then drop dead.

(DR HULL *gets up, walks across the row, and sits next to* MONDO.)

DR HULL: I wanted to thank you for your letter.

MONDO: You're welcome.

DR HULL: It was very well-written, you know.

MONDO: Van Gogh helped me with that.

DR HULL: I didn't deserve it.

MONDO: Of course you did. You're a wonderful doctor.

DR HULL: Wonderful's not the word I'd use. Neither is doctor.

MONDO: Did they take away your license?

DR HULL: I begged them not to.

MONDO: For good?

DR HULL: It's suspended for the length of my probation.

MONDO: How long is that?

DR HULL: Five years.

MONDO: That's not bad.

DR HULL: It's better than it could have been. I had to confess everything to the Judge. My lawyer forced me to. In front of everybody. With my ma sitting right there. I didn't want her to hear all that. She hasn't seen the Reading papers. She's allergic to the ink. She can only read *USA Today* without sneezing.

MONDO: What did you say?

DR HULL: That I was sorry.

MONDO: For what?

DR HULL: Abusing my privileges as a doctor. Abusing. A lot.

MONDO: That's what happened. That's O K. It's good that you said all that. *(Pause)* What happens now?

DR HULL: Twenty-four hour urine collection. I have to stay in treatment. If that's possible.

MONDO: Of course, is possible.

DR HULL: I don't know.

MONDO: Why not?

DR HULL: I don't know.

MONDO: There are people trained for this. I mean they won't get insulted no matter what you say to them. They know how to behave, they know what sentences to give you, they have them memorized. You can disappear at one of those places, rest, and come back.

DR HULL: Come back to what?

MONDO: Who knows? Something different.

(Pause. DR HULL kisses MONDO.)

MONDO: It started snowing, you know.

DR HULL: Already?

MONDO: It must be thirties outside. Below zero.

DR HULL: Not below zero.

MONDO: Below thirty-two is below zero. *(Pause)* Is coming down like dollar signs. And now that I have both eyes, I can see it how it really is. The snowflakes, the space between the snowflakes. It's something isn't it? Water that becomes into snow. It starts out as a drop, then comes through different layers of atmosphere and takes the shape of a doily. It's very exciting when the snow is falling, especially the first time, before the dead winter when you get frost bites. The pavement outside looks so good with that snow on top of it. *(Pause)* I forgot there could be something so beautiful, that I could be surrounded by something so beautiful, that it could come down and touch me.

(DR HULL *stirs. They get up and walk through the back exit. The double doors of the theater close behind them.*)

END OF PLAY